Little Essays Toward Truth

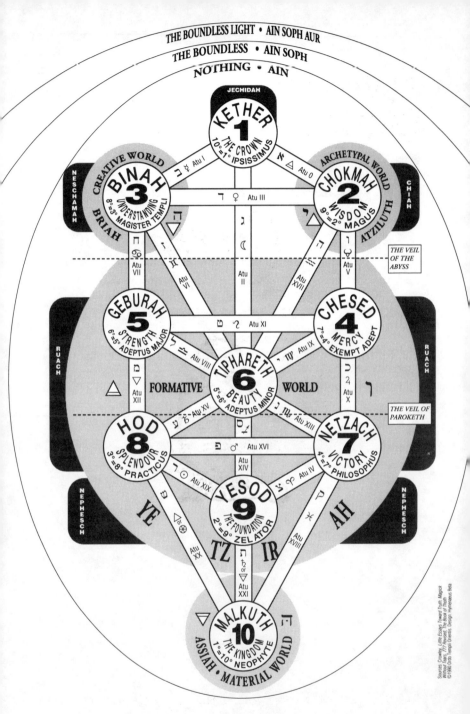

THE BOUNDLESS LIGHT • AIN SOPH AUR
THE BOUNDLESS • AIN SOPH
NOTHING • AIN

עץ חיים   THE TREE OF LIFE

The Three Veils of the Negative • The Ten Sephiroth with their Numbers, Names, Titles and Grades
The Veils of the Abyss and of Paroketh • The 22 Paths with their Tarot, Elemental, Planetary, Zodiacal and Hebrew correspondences
The Fivefold Constitution of Man • The Tetragrammaton in the Four Worlds

Sources: Crowley, Little Essays Toward Truth, Magick
Without Tears, 777 Revised, The Book of Thoth
©1990 Ordo Templi Orientis; Design: Hymenaeus Beta

ALEISTER
CROWLEY

Little
Essays
Toward
Truth

NEW FALCON PUBLICATIONS
SCOTTSDALE ❦ 1991 EV

Ordo Templi Orientis

First edition published privately by
Ordo Templi Orientis, London, 1938 EV.

Second revised edition.

Editorial and production supervision:
Fra. Superior Ὑμεναιος B
Fra. Φωτοσ

Ordo Templi Orientis
Publications Office
JAF Box 7666
New York, NY 10116-4632

ISBN 0-56184-000-9

1 3 5 7 9 10 8 6 4 2

New Falcon Publications
7025 East First Avenue, Suite 5
Scottsdale, AZ 85251

Contents

A∴A∴
Publication in Class B.

Foreword
to the Second Edition

IN THE HERMETIC TRADITION, as in the Zoharic Qabalah, the initiate perceives the harmonies and correspondences that govern the inner and outer worlds. By their mastery he perfects his soul and ascends mystically in the hierarchy of creation to rule over Nature. At the turn of the last century, this doctrine was epitomized in an English magical fraternity, the Hermetic Order of the Golden Dawn, where Aleister Crowley received his early magical training.

Aleister Crowley's Magick derives from these sources, with a forward-looking modernity imparted by the prophetic text *The Book of the Law*, the source of the Law of Thelema: "Do what thou wilt shall be the whole of the Law." As foreseen by Giordano Bruno centuries before the dawn of the New Æon, Thelema is a theurgy rooted in antiquity but compatible with scientific progress. Its esoterism is global, embracing Yoga, Buddhism, Qabalah, Sufism, Taoism and other non-European religious disciplines. Thelema is not alone in giving philosophical voice to the universal truths all religious systems possess. But it speaks from the standpoint of a truly Western spirituality that is only now emerging from the darkness of centuries of Christian suppression.

Crowley had another precursor in the Renaissance encyclopedist Giovanni Pico della Mirandola, who transformed Western magic by wedding Neoplatonism's Hermetic "doctrine of correspondences" to the Hebrew Qabalah. Both men were profoundly influenced by the *Chaldæan Oracles*, a collection of precepts attributed to Zoroaster collated by the Byzantine philosopher Michael Psellus in the eleventh century EV. Crowley considered *Little Essays Toward Truth* to be "a species of Commentary thereupon."

The present volume was first published privately by Ordo Templi Orientis in 1938 EV. For this second revised edition, an index has been added, together with a bibliography that includes works cited and suggested readings.

Had Aleister Crowley been invited to give Harvard's Norton Lectures, he might well have delivered these essays. They are perhaps the finest examples in the English language of the expository power of theoretical Qabalah.

HYMENAEUS BETA
Frater Superior, O.T.O.

The Mind of the Father
riding on the subtle guiders
which glitter with the inflexible tracings
of relentless fire.

ZOROASTER

Man

What is man, that thou art mindful of him?

M AN being the subject of these Essays, it is first proper to explain what will be meant therein by the word.

Man is a microcosm: that is, an image (concentrated around the point of consciousness) of the macrocosm, or Universe. This Theorem is guaranteed by the hylo-idealistic demonstration that the perceptible Universe is an extension, or phantasm, of the nervous system.

It follows that all phenomena, internal and external, may be classified for the purpose of discussing their observed relations, in any manner which experience may show to be the most convenient. (Examples: the elaborate classifications of science, chemical, physical, *etc., etc.* There is no essential truth in any of these aids to thinking: convenience is the sole measure.) Now for the purposes of analysing the spiritual nature of man, of recording and measuring his experiences in this kind, of planning his progress to loftier heights of attainment, several systems have been devised. That of the *Abhidhamma* is on the surface alike the most practical, the most scientific, and the most real; but for European students it is certainly far too unwieldy, to say nothing of other lines of criticism.

Therefore, despite the danger of vagueness involved in the use of a system whose terms are largely symbolic, I have, for many reasons, preferred to present to the world as an international basis for classification, the classico-mathematical system which is vulgarly and erroneously (though conveniently) called the Qabalah.

The Qabalah, that is, the Jewish Tradition concerning the initiated interpretation of their Scriptures, is mostly either unintelligible or nonsense. But it contains as its ground-plan the most precious jewel of human thought, that geometrical arrangement of names and numbers which is called the Tree of Life. I call it most precious, because I have found it the most convenient method hitherto discovered of classifying the phenomena of the Universe, and recording their relations. Whereof the proof is the amazing fertility of thought which has followed my adoption of this scheme.

Since all phenomena soever may be referred to the Tree of Life (which may be multiplied or subdivided at will for convenience's sake) it is evidently useless to attempt any complete account of it. The correspondences of each unit—the Ten Sephiroth and the Two-and-Twenty Paths—are infinite. The art of using it consists principally in referring all our ideas to it, discovering thus the common nature of certain things and the essential differences between others, so that ultimately one obtains a simple view of the incalculably vast complexity of the Universe.

The whole subject must be studied in the Book *777*, and the main attributions committed to memory: then when by constant use the system is at last understood—as opposed to being merely memorised—the student will find fresh light break in on him at every turn as he continues to measure every item of new knowledge that he attains by this Standard. For to him the Universe will then begin to appear as a coherent and a necessary Whole.

For the purpose of studying these Little Essays, it will be sufficient if a bare outline of the Cosmic Theory which they imply be given: but it may be added that, the fuller the comprehension of the Tree of Life which the reader brings to them, the clearer will their thought appear, and the more cogent their conclusions.

The Constitution of Man is fivefold.

(1) *Jechidah.*

This is the quintessential principle of the Soul, that which makes man at the same time identical with every other spark of Godhead, and different (as regards his point-of-view, and the Universe of which it is the centre) from all others. It is a Point, possessing only position;

11

and that position is only definable by reference to co-ordinate axes, to secondary principles, which only pertain to it *per accidens,* and must be postulated as our conception grows.

(2) *Chiah.*

This is the Creative Impulse or Will of Jechidah, the energy which demands the formulation of the co-ordinate axes aforesaid, so that Jechidah may obtain self-realisation, a formal understanding of what is implicit in its nature, of its possible qualities.

(3) *Neschamah.*

This is the faculty of understanding the Word of Chiah. It is the intelligence or intuition of what Jechidah wishes to discover about itself.

These three principles constitute a Trinity; they are *one,* because they represent the being, and the apparatus which will make the manifestation possible, of a God, in manhood. But they are only, so to speak, the mathematical structure of man's nature. One might compare them with the laws of physics, as they are before they are discovered. There are as yet no data by whose examination they may be discerned.

A conscious man, accordingly, cannot possibly know anything of these three principles, although they constitute his essence. It is the work of Initiation to *journey inwards* to them. See, in the Oath of a Probationer of A∴A∴

"I pledge myself to discover the nature and powers of my own Being."

This triune principle being wholly spiritual, all that can be said about it is really negative. And it is complete in itself. Beyond it stretches what is called The Abyss. This doctrine is extremely difficult to explain; but it corresponds more or less to the gap in thought between the Real, which is ideal, and the Unreal, which is actual. In the Abyss all things exist, indeed, at least *in posse*, but are without any possible meaning; for they lack the substratum of spiritual Reality. They are appearances without Law. They are thus *Insane Delusions*.

Now the Abyss being thus the great storehouse of Phenomena, it is the source of all impressions. And the Triune Principle has intented a *machine* for investigating the Universe; and this machine is the fourth Principle of Man.

(4) *Ruach*.

This may be translated Mind, Spirit, or Intellect: none of these is satisfactory, the connotation varying with every writer. The Ruach is a closely-knitted group of Five Moral and Intellectual principles, concentrated on their core, Tiphareth, the Principle of Harmony, the Human Consciousness and Will of which the four other Sephiroth are (so to speak) the feelers. And these five principles culminate in a sixth, Daäth, Knowledge. But this is not really a principle; it contains in itself the germ of self-contradiction and so of self-destruction. It is a false principle: for, as soon as Knowledge is analysed, it breaks up into the irrational dust of the Abyss.

Man's aspiration to Knowledge is thus simply a false road: it is to spin ropes of sand.

We cannot here enter into the doctrine of the "Fall of Adam," invented to explain in parable how it is that the Universe is so unfortunately constituted. We are concerned only with the observed facts.

All these mental and moral faculties of the Ruach, while not purely spiritual like the Supernal Triad, are still, as it were, "in the air." To be of use, they need a basis through which to receive impressions, much as a machine requires fuel and fodder before it can manufacture the article which it is designed to produce.

(5) *Nephesch.*

This is usually translated the "Animal Soul." It is the vehicle of the Ruach, the instrument by which the Mind is brought into contact with the dust of Matter in the Abyss, that it may feel it, judge it, and react to it. This is itself a principle still spiritual, in a sense; the actual body of man is composed of the dust of Matter, temporarily held together by the Principles which inform it, for their own pur-

14

poses, and ultimately for the supreme purpose of self-realisation of Jechidah.

But Nephesch, devised as it is with no other object than the direct traffic with Matter, tends to partake of its incoherence. Its faculties of perceiving pain and pleasure lure it into paying undue attention to one set of phenomena, into shunning another. Hence, for the Nephesch to do its work as it should, it requires to be dominated by the severest discipline. Nor is the Ruach itself to be trusted in this matter. It has its own tendencies to weakness and injustice. It tries every trick—and it is diabolically clever—to arrange its business with Matter in the sense most convenient to its inertia, without the smallest consideration of its duty to the Supernal Triad, cut off as that is from its comprehension; indeed, unsuspecting as it normally is of its existence.

What then determines Tiphareth, the Human Will, to aspire to comprehend Neschamah, to submit itself to the divine Will of Chiah?

Nothing but the realisation, born sooner or later of agonising experience, that its whole relation through Ruach and Nephesch with Matter, *i.e.*, with the Universe, is, and must be, only painful. The senselessness of the whole procedure sickens it. It begins to seek for some menstruum in which the Universe may become

15

intelligible, useful and enjoyable. In Qabalistic language, it aspires to Neschamah.

This is what we mean in saying that the Trance of Sorrow is the motive of the Great Work.

This "Trance of Sorrow" (which must be well distinguished from any petty personal despair, any "conviction of sin," or other black magical imitations) being cosmic in scope, comprehending all phenomena actual or potential, is then already an Opening of the Sphere of Neschamah. The awareness of one's misfortune is itself an indication of the remedy. It sets the seeker on the right road, and as he develops his Neschamah he soon attains other Experiences of this high order. He learns the meaning of his own true Will, to pronounce his own Word, to identify himself with Chiah.

Finally, realising Chiah as the dynamic aspect of Jechidah, he becomes that pure Being, at once universal and individual, equally nothing, One, and All.

It is of the essence of the Ideas of the Supernal Triad that the Laws of Reason which apply to intellectual functions are no longer operative. Hence it is impossible to convey the nature of these Experiences in rational language. Further, their scope is infinite in every direction, so that it would be futile to attempt to enumerate or to describe them in detail. All that one can do is to note the common types in very general language, and to indicate what experience has shewn to be the most useful main lines of research.

The Quest of the Holy Grail, the Search for the Stone of the Philosophers—by whatever name we choose to call the Great Work—is therefore endless. Success only opens up new avenues of brilliant possibility. Yea, verily, and Amen! the task is tireless and its joys without bounds; for the whole Universe, and all that in it is, what is it but the infinite playground of the Crowned and Conquering Child, of the insatiable, the innocent, the ever-rejoicing Heir of Space and Eternity, whose name is MAN?

Memory

MEMORY is of the very stuff of Consciousness itself. Consider that we can never know *what is happening,* but only *what has just happened,* even when most actively concentrated on what we call "the present."

Moreover, no impression short of Sammasamadhi can ever pretend to confer any coherent idea of the Self. That exists only in an order of Consciousness far deeper than direct perception, in a type of thought which is capable of combining the quintessence of countless impressions into one, as also of transforming this *tabula rasa* into a positive prehensile Ego. Whether this process be hallucinatory or no, it is surely memory which, more than any other function of the mind, determines its possibilities.

Now, whatever view we may take of the nature of the Self, it is clear that our limit of error will constantly diminish as the range of our observations is extended. To calculate the orbit of Neptune from a period of days when it is retrograde could lead to formidable fallacies. When memory is seriously weakened, the resulting state approximates to dementia. Memory is then, in a figure, the mortar of the architecture of the mind.

It seems impossible even to begin to discuss its nature as it is in itself; for it is not a Thing at all, but only a relation between impressions. We must be content to observe its virtues.

First of all is that already noted, its extent in time. Second is the faculty of selection.

It would be as undesirable as it is impossible for the memory to retain all impressions indiscriminately. Such memories are found only in lunatic asylums. The memory, whatever it may be, depends on cerebral metabolism; and it thrives on a proper harmony of exercise, repose, and economy just as does muscular strength.

Memory as such is practically worthless; it is like an abandoned library. Its data must be co-ordinated by judgment, and played upon with skill; it resembles a great Organ which requires an organist.

By classifying simple impressions, one obtains ideas of a higher order; the repetition of this process gives a structure to the mind which makes it a worthy instrument of thought. And this means enables one to retain, and to bring at will from their quiet resting-place, a thousandfold the number of facts which would overwhelm the untrained memory. One must model one's mind upon the arrangement of the ends of the nerve-fibres and the brain.

At will! Here is the great key to proper selection, that one should resolutely remember all facts that may be useful, and as resolutely forget all those impertinent, to the True Way of one's Star in Space. For so only can one economise the mnemonic faculty; and this is to say: no man can begin to train his memory duly until he is aware of his True Will.

There is then—as in all matters pertaining to the intellect—a vicious circle: for one can only become conscious of one's True Will by a judgment (of Samadhic intensity) upon all facts that it is possible to assimilate. The resolution of the antinomy is found *ambulando*: that is by the selective training above indicated.

A further complication of this whole question appears during the practice of Yoga, when, the sheaths being successively stripped from the mind, one begins to remember not only long-forgotten facts, but matters which do not refer to the incarnated Ego at all. The memory extends in time to infancy, to one's previous death, and so further to an unlimited series of experiences whose scope depends on the degree of one's progress. But, parallel with this intensification of the idea of the Ego, its expansion through the æons, there arises (in consequence of the weakening of the Ahamkara, the Ego-making faculty) a tendency to remember things which have happened not to "oneself," but to "other people" or beings.

Herein is one of the most irritating obstacles in the Path of the Wise; for the normal development of the memory in Time leads to a better understanding of the True Will of the individual (as he then conceives of himself) so that he perceives an universe teleologically more rational as he progresses. To be compelled to assimilate the experiences of supposed "alien beings" is to become confused: the old hotchpot of Choronzon (Restriction be unto him in the name of BABALON!) gapes once more for the Adept, who possibly supposed himself already (in a sense) a Freeman of the City of the Pyramids.

But it is just this experience—in default of any other—which eventually insists on his undertaking to cross the Abyss: for the alternative to sheer insanity is seen to be the discovery of a General Formula comprehensive of Universal Experience without reference to the Ego (real or supposed) in any sense.

This paradox, like all others, should be a lesson of supreme value: this, that every difficulty is for our vantage, that every question is posed only in order to lead us to an answer involving a triumph infinitely more glorious than we could otherwise have conceived.

And meditation upon this whole matter may not unlikely bring us to this further vision of Wonder: that the nature of things themselves is in reality but a function of Memory.

Sorrow

THE ASPIRATION to become a Master is rooted in the Trance of Sorrow.

This trance is not simple and definite; indeed, it commonly begins in a limited selfish form.

The imagination cannot pierce beyond terrestrial conditions, or the sense of self grasp more than the natural consciousness.

One thinks at first no more than this: "there is nothing possible that is good enough for me." Only as one grows by Initiation does one approach the asymptote "sabbé pi Dukkham"* of the Buddha, when the relations of subject and object, both expanded to infinity, are seen to be no less in the bosom of the Great Curse than were their first avatars, the petty Ego and the perceptible Universe.

So also for the transcending of this Trance of Sorrow. At first the victory often comes by trick of mind; extending subject or object, as the case may be, by an effort to escape reality, one seems for a moment to have defeated the Equation "Everything is Sorrow"; but the clouds regather as the mind recovers its equilibrium. Thus, one invents some "Heaven," defining it

---

* ["Everything is Sorrow"]

arbitrarily as free from sorrow: only to find, on exact examination, that its conditions are the same as those of "Earth."

Nor is there any rational issue from this hell of thought. The transcending of the Trance of Sorrow is to be made by means of such other trances as the Higher Beatific Vision, the Trance of Wonder, and others, even the Trance called the Universal Joke, though this last is thereunto strangely akin!

There is this further consideration; that every subject of contemplation asks only that the mind should become fixed upon it, in a degree far inferior to that of true concentration such as secures Samadhi, to become evidently an illusion.

So much for a brief summary of the technical aspects of the matter. But all this is remote indeed from the simplicity of the affirmation of *The Book of the Law*:

> Remember all ye that existence is pure joy; that all the sorrows are but as shadows; they pass & are done; but there is that which remains.

Upon what can depend this perception, which claims to sweep away with the fire of scorn the formidable batteries of all serious philosophical thought? The solution must lie in the metaphysics of Thelema itself.

And here we come upon what is apparently a paradox of the most disconcerting order. For *The Book of the Law*, anticipating the most subtle of recent mathematical conceptions, that of the greatest genius of this generation, makes the unit of existence consist in an Event, an Act of Marriage between Nuit and Hadit; that is, the fulfilment of a certain Point-of-View. And is not the procession of events the very condition of Sorrow as opposed to the perfection of "Pure Existence?" That is the old philosophy, a tangle of false words: we see more clearly. Thus:

Each Event is an Act of Love, and so generates Joy: all existence is composed solely of such Events. But how comes it then that there should be even an illusion of Sorrow?

Simply enough; by taking a partial and imperfect Vision. An example: in the human body each cell is perfect, and the man is in good health; but should we choose to regard almost any portion of the machine which sustains him, there will appear various decompositions and the like, which might well be taken to imply the most tragic Events. And this would inevitably be the case had we never at any time seen the man as a whole, and understood the necessity of the divers processes of nature which combine to make life.

Furthermore, to the normal or dualistic consciousness it is precisely the shadows which

"pass & are done" which constitute percepti-
bility: what man "sees" is in fact just that which
obstructs the rays of light. This is the justification for the Buddha saying: "Everything is
Sorrow": in that word "Everything" he is most
careful to include specifically all those things
which men count joyous. And this is not really
a paradox; for to him all reactions which produce consciousness are ultimately sorrowful, as
being disturbances of the Perfection of Peace,
or (if you prefer it) as obstructions to the free
flow of Energy.

Joy and Sorrow are thus to him relative
terms; subdivisions of one great sorrow, which
is manifestation. We need not trouble to con-
test this view; indeed, the "Shadows" of
which our book speaks are those interfer-
ences with Light caused by the partiality of
our apprehension.

The Whole is Infinite Perfection, and so is
each Unit thereof. To transcend the Trance of
Sorrow it is thus sufficient to cancel the subject of the contemplation by marrying it to its
equal and opposite in imagination. We may
also pursue the analytical method, and resolve the complex which appears Sorrow into
its atoms. Each event of it is a sublime and
joyous act of Love; or the synthetical method,
proceeding from the part to the Whole, with
a similar result.

And any one of the movements of the mind is (with assiduity and enthusiasm) capable of transforming the Trance of Sorrow itself into the cognate Trance attributed to Understanding, the Trance of Wonder.

Wonder

"**A** LITTLE MORE than kin, and less than kind" are the Trance of Sorrow, and the Vision of the Machinery of the Universe; this latter being the technical aspect of the Apprehension of the Law of Change, which is also a Trance of the same order as that of Sorrow. Now one mode of victory over all these is the Trance of Indifference, in which one stands aloof from the whole matter; but it is only one mode, and (in the generally known form) full of falsehood and imperfection. For to stand aloof is to affirm duality, which is itself the root of Sorrow. To obtain the highest one must unite oneself with all things, partake of all as a true Sacrament. And this motion leads to the Trance of Wonder.

It is written "The fear of the Lord is the Beginning of Wisdom." Here the Predicate refers to the Opening of the Grade of Magus; but the Subject, duly translated, reads "The Wondering at Tetragrammaton," and so refers to this Trance. For herein one is wholly identified with the Universe in its dynamic aspect; and the first synthesis of the understanding thereof is this Amazement at the fitness and necessity of the entire mechanism. For, given the formula of Manifestation, the need to conceive and perceive Perfection by means of the symbolism of Imperfection, the actual process of ideation becomes apodeictic. (I write as for the least instructed of the Little Children of the Light.)

The Trance of Wonder arises naturally—it is the first movement of the mind—from the final phrase of the Oath of a Master of the Temple. "I will interpret every phenomenon as a particular dealing of God with my soul." For, immediately the Understanding illuminates the darkness of knowledge, every fact appears in its true guise miraculous.

It is so: then, how marvellous that it should so be!

In all Trances of importance, and most especially in this, the Postulant should have acquired the greatest possible knowledge and Understanding of the Universe properly so called. His rational mind should have been trained thoroughly in intellectual apprehension: that is, he should be familiar with all Science. This is evidently impossible on the face of it; but he should aspire to the closest approximation to perfect Adeptship in this matter. The method most possible is to make a detached study of some chosen branch of one Science, and a general study of epistemology. Then by analogy, fortified by contemplation, a certain inner apprehension of the Unity of Nature may grow up in the mind, one which will not be unduly presumptuous and misleading.

But our Work demands more than this. The Neschamah or Intuitive Mind must also be furnished with Knowledge and Understanding of those Planes of Nature which are inaccessible to the untrained sense. That is, he must pursue our Methods of Vision with indefatigable ardour.

Now in all this the true unitive and transcendental Science is that of Mathematics for the Ruach, and its crown the Holy Qabalah for the Neschamah. By this means the Work is not, as would at first seem, increased beyond human capability. There is a definite critical stage, comparable to that familiar to the Adepts of Asana and of Dharana, after which the terms of the Equation (like the latter terms of a Binomial Expansion) repeat themselves, though after another manner, so that the meditation becomes progressively easier. The Postulant, so to speak, finds himself at home. The added knowledge is no longer a burden to the mind. He is able to throw off the gross facts which present themselves as complications, and to apprehend their essence in simplicity. He has in fact succeeded in developing a higher function of the mind. The process is similar to that which occurs in ordinary study of a science, when one, by grasping the nature of a general law underlying diversity of experience, is able not only to assimilate new facts with ease, but to predict new facts wholly unknown. One may instance the discovery of Neptune from mathematical considerations without optical research, and the description of unknown elements by contemplation of the Periodic Law.

Let it be known that each such step in Meditation is itself a motive Energy capable of inducing the Trance of Wonder; and this Trance (like all others) grows in sublimity and splendour with the quantity and quality of the material which is furnished to the mind by the Adept.

Those, therefore, who effect to despise "profane" Science are themselves despicable. It is their own incapacity for true Thought of any serious kind, their vanity and pertness; nay more also! their own subconscious sense of their own shame and idleness, that induces them to build these flimsy fortifications of pretentious ignorance.

There is nothing in the Universe which is not of supreme significance, nothing which may not be used as the very keystone of the Rainbow Arch of the Trance of Wonder.

It is necessary to add but one brief word to this elementary essay: this Trance is of its nature not only passive and intuitive. Its occurrence floods the mind with Creative Energy; it fills the Adept with Power, and excites in him the Will to work. It exalts him to the Atziluthic World in his Essence, and in his manifestation to the Briatic. In a very special

LITTLE ESSAYS TOWARD TRUTH

sense, therefore, it may be said that the Postulant is most intimately united with the Supreme Lord God Most High, the True and Living Creator of all Things, whensoever he attains to enter this most Majestic Pylon of the Trance of Wonder.

Beatitude

THERE ARE TWO well-distinguished forms of the Beatific Vision. The higher pertains to Kether, and is thus proper only to the Ipsissimus, though it may be enjoyed sporadically (and, as it were, by accident) by those of lower grades.

It is of extremely rare occurrence, and has indeed never been described in any detail; it may even be said that it is doubtful whether any account of its true form has ever been given to the world. It need only be said in this place that its formula is "Love is the law, love under will," and that its nature is the Perpetual Sacrament of Energy in action. It is dependent upon the perfect mastery of the Mysteries of Sorrow and of Change, with thorough identification with that of Individuality.

Let us then occupy ourselves with the lower form of this Vision (so called; it is not technically a Vision at all) which pertains to Tiphareth, and is thus the natural grace of the Minor Adept. It may be said at once that those who have attained to higher grades, especially those above the Abyss, can hardly return to this Vision. For it implies a certain innocence, a certain defect of Understanding which is not possible to a Master of the Temple. Again, the Grades of Exempt and Major Adept are too energetic to admit of the balanced quietude of this state.

Only in the centre of the Tree of Life, only in the self-poised security of the Solar Axis, can we expect to find the steady indifference to Event which is the basis of the Trance, and that ontogenous radiance which tinges it with Rose and Gold.

This Trance differs notably from most others in a way which the above-stated conditions would lead us to expect. It is, psychologically, a state; as opposed to an Action or an Event. True, all Trances of Samadhic intensity are in a sense timeless; but it may be said that most of them are marked by well-defined issues of a critical character. That is, the entry to each is quasi-spasmodic.

In this case, however, we find no such diagnostic.

The Trance may be continued for weeks or months, and the most ardent devotee of Tahuti, searching his Magical Record with the most conscientious acuteness, finds it impossible to indicate the onset of the Vision. In fact, it may be surmised that the Vision arises not from any given action but rather from a subtle suspension of action. The conflict of events has ended happily in a state of serenely perfect balance, in which, though energy continues to manifest, its issues have become without significance. We may compare the condition with the return to health of a fever-stricken man. The alternation of pyrexia and sub-normal temperatures has subsided; he forgets gradually to consult the thermometer at the accustomed intervals, becoming absorbed instinctively in his regular pursuits. At the same time he is no longer aware of the hot and cold spells, but half consciously of the quiet glow of health. Similarly in this Vision all conscious magical effort ceases, although the practices are continued with all customary diligence, and the whole of the Adept's impressions, internal as external, are suffused with the glow of beauty and delight. The state is in many respects closely akin to that sought by the smoker of opium; but it is natural and requires no artificial regulation.

It will appear from the foregoing that nothing could be more absurd than to attempt to give instructions for the attainment of this state.

To aspire to it (still worse, to seek to regain it after it has passed) must appear the climax of bad logic. Nor, delectable and blessed as it is, can one call it actually desirable.

We need not assume that it is in any way deleterious, that it exhausts good Karma, or that it wastes time and damps aspiration. It should be accepted, when it occurs, with calm indifference, enjoyed to the full, and quitted without regret. Its occurrence is in any case clear evidence that the Adept has reached a definite and rather exalted state of being, since he can live so many hours without being perturbed by the incidence of any motive force. It implies a marked degree of attainment of internal and external control. It proves the possibility of perfect repose in the midst of the greatest activity, and thus indicates the solution of the ultimate problem of philosophy, the proem to the conquest of the Three Characteristics. It should encourage the Adept in his Aspiration by heartening him to confront the appalling postulate of the Abyss. It should serve him as refreshment and nourishment; it should assure him of the possibility of perfection in the Greater Work by demonstrating its existence as a Crown to the Less.

Moreover, the enjoyment of Delight and the apprehension of Beauty in all things, even on this plane where analysis has not yet become acute, do actually fortify the heart and enkindle the imagination.

Let therefore the Postulant of the Rosy Cross pursue his Path in solemn strength, aware that at the proper moment he may receive, unasking, the reward, and enjoy the revivifying flood of dulcet Light, which has been called by the Adepts the Beatific Vision.

Laughter

THE COMMON DEFECT of all mystical systems previous to that of the Æon whose Law is Thelema is that there has been no place for Laughter. But the sadness of the mournful Mother and the melancholy of the dying Man are swept into the limbo of the past by the confident smile of the immortal Child.

And there is no Vision more critical in the career of the Adept of Horus than the Universal Joke.

In this Trance he accepts fully the Formula of Osiris, and in the act transcends it; the spear of the Centurion passes harmlessly through his heart, and the sword of the Executioner strikes idly on his neck. He discovers that the Tragedy of which so many centuries have made such a case is but a farce for children's pleasure. Punch is knocked down only to get up grinning with his gay "Root-too-too-tit! Here we are again!" Judy, the Beadle, the Hangman and the Devil are merely the companions of his playtime.

So, since (after all) the facts which he thought tragic are real enough, the essence of his solution is that they are not true, as he thought, of himself; they are just one set of phenomena, as interesting and as fatuously impotent to affect him as any other set. His personal grief was due to his passionate insistence on contemplating one insignificant congeries of Events as if it were the sole reality and importance in the infinite mass of Manifestation.

It is thus that the Perception of the Universal Joke leads directly to the Understanding of the Idea of Self as conterminous with the Universe, and at the same time one with it, creator of it, and aloof from it; which Triune State is, as is well known, one of the most necessary stages of Samadhi. (It is the culmination of one of the two most important chapters of the *Bhagavadgita*.)

There is a further merit in this matter. In the idea of Laughter is inherent that of Cruelty, as has been shewn by many philosophers; and this is doubtless why it has been excluded by the Mystic Schools of Pitymongers from their dull curricula. The only answer is to shrug the shoulders in humorous contempt. For on this rock and no other have all their brave barks foundered one by one amid the 'ανηριθμον γελασμα* of Ocean. Nature is full of cruelty; its highest points of joy and victory are marked by laughter. It is the true physiological explosion and relaxation of a tension which produces it. Notably, such drugs as *Cannabis Indica* and *Anhalonium Lewinii*, which do actually "loosen the girders of the soul which give her breathing," cause

---

* ["countless smiles."]

immediate laughter as one of their most characteristic effects.

Oh the huge wholesome contempt for the limiting self which springs from the sense of Gargantuan disproportion perceived in this Laughter! Truly it slays, with jolliest cannibal revels, that sour black-coated missionary the serious Ego, and plumps him into the pot. Te-he!—the Voice of Civilisation—the Messenger of the White Man's God—bubble, bubble, bubble! Throw in another handful of sage, brother! And the sweet-smelling smoke rises and veils with exquisite shy seduction the shameless bodies of the Stars!

Beyond all this for practical value—since the signpost at every turn of the Path of the Wise reads DANGER—yet springing directly from it by virtue of this very slaying of the Ego, is the use of Laughter as a safeguard of sanity. How easy for the charlatans of oratory to seduce the simple enthusiasm of the soul! What help have we unless we have the wit to know them as ridiculous? There is no limit to the abyss of Idiocy wherein the quacks would plunge us— our only saving reflex is the automatic joke of the Sense of Humour!

Robert Browning was not far from the Kingdom of God when he wrote:

Rejoice that man is hurled
　From change to change unceasingly,
His soul's wings never furled

and there is after all but little salt in the sneer of Juvenal's "Satur est cum dicit Horatius 'Evohe!' "* For it is yet to be recorded that any man brought aid or comfort to his fellow by moping.

No, the Universal Joke, though it be not a true Trance, is most assuredly a means of Grace, and often proves the chief ingredient of the Universal Solvent.

Back then to Browning, to the brave last words he wrote while fourscore struck upon the timepiece of his years:

> Greet the unseen with a cheer!
> Bid him forward, breast and back as either
>   should be.
> 'Strive and thrive,' cry 'Speed, — fight on,
>   fare ever 'There as here!'

> Amen.

> Were the world understood,
>   Ye would see it was good,
> A dance to a delicate measure!

Ay! let us end with that most sudden surprising Word of a certain Angel of *The Vision and the Voice*, who left the Seer lapsed in his solemn Trance with the gay laughing phrase— "But I go dancing!"

The Tables of the Law? Bah! *Solvuntur tabulæ!—risu!* †

---

* ["Horace was well-sated when he cried 'Evohè.' "]
† ["Let the Tables be broken! — with Laughter!"]

Indifference

THE STATE OF MIND which is characterised by Indifference is commonly called Trance, but the misnomer is unfortunate. It is, in fact, in a sense the precise contrary of a Trance; for Trance usually implies Samadhi, and this state specifically excludes any such occurrence. That implies a uniting, and this a willed dissociation. Yet there is nothing herein to suggest necessarily any practice of the Black Brothers; for it is not, properly speaking, an Attainment, but rather a convenient attitude. And it is one of the very greatest practical importance and use. One can not remain indefinitely in any Samadhi; at the same time, it is proper to fill the intervals between gusts of positive work in such a way as to leave oneself as free as possible to take the next step. One should therefore cultivate a habit of mind which is not bound by any form of desire. The State of Indifference is thus a form of that Silence which is defence and protection, and is cognate with the Third Noble Truth of Buddhism, Sorrow's Ceasing.

The general idea of the state is that the mind should react automatically to each and every impression: "It does not matter whether the Event be ay or nay." Blavatsky observes that the feeling is at least tinged with disgust. But this is an error; such a state is imperfect. There should, on the contrary, be a quite definite joy, not in the impression itself but in being indifferent to it. This joy springs doubtless from the sense of power involved; but that is again an imperfection; one should rather rejoice in the cognizance of the ultimate truth that "existence is pure joy," not in any feeling more immediate.

It is to be observed that the attainment and maintenance of this state depends to a great extent on the mastery of several Trances. For instance, one must be convinced of the First Noble Truth by the Trance of Sorrow, or it would not be logical to be indifferent to all things; there might be, in the absence of this perception of "sabbè pi Dukkham," some impression which actually led to some state free from Sorrow, and this is not the case. Freedom from Sorrow depends on freedom from impression.

Yet it would not be fair to say that this State of Indifference was akin to that Dullness which succeeds the acute spasm of Sorrow; it is not the anæsthesia of a nerve worn out by excess of pain. There is never any place in the curriculum of a Magician for passivity—of course we here except what may be called the Active or Willed Passivity described in *Liber LXV*. Indifference is to be an intensely active condition. One may compare it with the ease of a skilled fencer, who meets and deflects every possible attack of his antagonist with equal vigour, unconscious of his acts, because he has trained his eye, wrist, and even his blade to think for themselves. Thus Indifference is the spiritual form of the Automatic Consciousness of the Adept; and this resides in Yesod, the place of the Fortress on the Frontier of the Abyss, as described in *Liber 418* in the Eleventh Æthyr.

This Indifference being a habit of Normal Mind, it is easier to attain than any true Samadhic State, and involves less technical ability. This is particularly the case because, as noted above, the Trance of Sorrow has been an almost necessary preliminary to the proper understanding of what it implies. The method therefore of acquiring (the word is to be preferred to "attaining") Indifference is simple; it is, in effect, the Way of the Tao.

The following Sorites may prove useful to the Aspirant:

> Existence is only to be understood as a Continuum.
> All parts of Existence are therefore ultimately equivalent, each being equally necessary to complete the whole.
> Each event is thus to be received with equal honour, and the reaction to it made with equal indifference.

To offer a practical parallel. Suppose one is to receive a thousand pounds, and this amount is paid over in divers coins, with I.O.U.'s for various sums. Since one knows in advance that the balance in one's favour is £1,000, one does not get excited on the appearance of any particular item, but goes on steadily counting, making the right reaction, whether a plus or a minus item is at issue, with perfect calm and accuracy. Each entry in the account may be different; but one's mental attitude is invariable. The common error of the unphilosophical mind is indeed due to ignorance of the true nature of the soul. One is apt to suppose that each Event as it occurs may be "good" or "bad," may indicate that one is winning or losing. But as soon as one is certain that the issue is factitious, that it has been determined beforehand, it becomes absurd to be affected by one incident in the illusory process which Nature uses symbolically to express the fatality of Truth rather than by any other.

It is interesting to note that this method of acquiring Indifference is quite independent of any experience of the Trance of Sorrow; it is a simple and normal consideration based on strictly Thelemic premisses. It is thus most highly to be recommended. The methods of the dead Æon of Osiris were in fact attended with no inconsiderable danger. The question of Separateness from the Universe is critical, for one thing; for another, it is a mistake to be dependent on such a theory as that implied in the First Noble Truth in its outer aspects. It is altogether better to adopt the purely intellectual attitude, and anchor it subsequently in Neschamah by simply transcending the normal rational mind in the usual way by the Method of Contradiction, or equating of Opposites, such as is described in *Konx Om Pax*, and in the best Essays on the Holy Qabalah.

It is apt, moreover, to lead to several types of error to regard Indifference as a state inferior to Samadhi. In particular one may tend to think of it as passive, as imperfect, as an interregnum; whereas it should be considered as a state of Peace with Victory.

It need only be added, in conclusion, that Indifference is not perfect until it has entered into full possession of at least one Samadhic trait, Automatism. As long as there remains any need of conscious effort in dealing with any impression, any need to remember the process by which the state is reached, or even any need of conscious interference with, or cognizance of, the purely spontaneous elastic reflex reaction, the Aspirant to the Summum Bonum, True Wisdom and Perfect Happiness, has not adequately acquired the Habit of Indifference.

Mastery

THE AIM of him who would be Master is single; men call it Personal Ambition. That is, he wants his Universe to be as vast, and his control of it as perfect, as possible.

Few fail to understand this aim; but many fail in the formulation of their campaign to attain it. Some, for instance, fill their purse with fairy gold, which, when they try to use it, is found to be dead leaves. Others attempt to rule the universe of another, not seeing that they cannot even take true cognizance thereof.

The proper method of extending one's universe, besides the conventional apparatus of material Science, is tripartite: evocation, invocation, and vision. Control is a matter of theoretical and practical acquaintance with Magical Formulæ, but notably also of Self-Discipline. The ground is to be consolidated, and all contradictions resolved in higher harmonies, by the various Trances.

So much indeed is obvious to superficial consideration; strange, then, that so few Magicians take the further step of enquiry as to the availability of the Instrument. Shortsighted selfishness, good sooth, to take for granted that one's Self is sure to find its proper medium to hand for its next adventure.

Here the Magical Memory is of virtue marvellous to correct perspective; for, how often in
the past has one's life been all but sheer failure
from the mere lack of proper means of self-
expression? And who among us can be seriously
satisfied (to-day, knowing what we do) with
even the most perfect human instrument?

It is then no more than simple good sense
for the Magus to formulate his general political
aim in some such terms as these:

> To secure the greatest possible freedom of
> self-expression for the greatest possible
> number of Points-of-View.

Of which issue the practical aspect may be
phrased as follows:

> To improve the human race in every con-
> ceivable way, so as to have available for ser-
> vice the greatest possible variety of the best
> Instruments imaginable.

And this is the rational justification of the apparently imbecile and too often sentimental-
hypocritical aphorism:

> Love all Beings! Serve Mankind!

That is, upon the political plane: for also these
two phrases contain (1) the Magical Formula
which is the Key alike of Invocation and of
Trance (2) the implicit injunction to make
clear the Way of the Magician through the
Heavens by right ordering of every Star.
The word "serve" is indeed misleading and

objectionable: it implies a false and despicable attitude. The relation between men should be the brotherly respect which obtains between noble strangers. The idea of service is either true, and humiliating; or false, and arrogant.

The most common and fatal pitfall which menaces the man who has begun to extend his Universe beyond the world of sense-perception is called Confusion of the Planes. To him who realises the All-One, and knows that to distinguish between any two things is the basic error, it must seem natural and even right to perform what seem perforce Acts of Love between incongruous ideas. He has the Key of Languages: why then should not he the Englishman avail himself of it to speak in Hebrew without learning it? The same problem offers itself daily in a myriad subtle shapes. "Command these stones to become bread." "Throw thyself down from the pinnacle of the Temple: as it is written 'He shall give his angels charge over thee, to keep thee in all thy ways.'"—These last four words throw light upon the fog of Choronzon—Restriction be unto him in the Name of BABALON! For "his ways" are the ways of Nature, who hath appointed between the planes a well-ordered relation; to deform this device is not, and cannot be, "thy way." The Act of Love, so-seeming, is a false gesture; for such love is not "love under will." Be thou well aware, O thou who seekest to attain to Mastery, of doing aught "miraculous":

the surest sign of the Master is this, that he is a man of like passions with his fellows. He does indeed transcend them all, and turn them all to perfections; but he does this without suppression (for "Everything that lives is holy") or distortion (for "Every Form is a true symbol of Substance") or confusion (for "Admixture is hatred as Union is love"). Initiation means The Journey Inwards: nothing is changed or can be changed; but all is trulier understood with every step. The Magus of the Gods, with His one Word that seems to overturn the chariot of Mankind in ruin, does not in fact destroy or even alter anything; He simply furnishes a new mode of applying existing Energy to established Forms.

The invention of electric machines has in no way interfered with Matter or Motion; it has only helped us to get rid of certain aspects of the Illusion of Time and Space, and so brought the most intelligent minds to the threshold of the Magical and Mystical Doctrine: they have been forced to imagine the possibility of the perception of the Universe as it is, freed of conditions. That is, they have been given a glimpse of the nature of the Attainment of Mastery. And it is surely but a little step to take for the leaders of natural Science, Mathematics their guiding Star, that they should understand the compelling necessity of the Great Work, and apply themselves to its achievement.

Here the great obstacles are these; firstly, the misunderstanding of Self; and secondly, the resistance of the rational mind against its own conclusions. Men must cast off these two restrictions; they must begin to realise that Self is hidden behind, and independent of, the mental and material instrument in which they apprehend their Point-of-View; and they must seek an instrument other than that which insists (with every single observation) on impressing on them what is merely its own most hateful flaw and error, the idea of duality.

The Æon of Horus is here: and its first flower may well be this: that, freed of the obsession of the doom of the Ego in Death, and of the limitation of the Mind by Reason, the best men again set out with eager eyes upon the Path of the Wise, the mountain track of the goat, and then the untrodden Ridge, that leads to the ice-gleaming pinnacles of Mastery!

Trance

THE WORD *Trance* implies a passing beyond: *scil.*, the conditions which oppress. The whole and sole object of all true Magical and Mystical training is to become free from every kind of limitation. Thus, body and mind, in the widest sense, are the obstacles in the Path of the Wise: the paradox, tragic enough as it seems, is that they are also the means of progress. How to get rid of them, to pass beyond or to transcend them, is the problem, and this is as strictly practical and scientific as that of eliminating impurities from a gas, or of adroitly using mechanical laws. Here is the inevitable logical flaw in the sorites of the Adept, that he is bound by the very principles which it is his object to overcome: and on him who seeks to discard them arbitrarily they haste to take a terrible revenge!

It is in practice, not in theory, that this difficulty suddenly disappears. For when we take rational steps to suspend the operation of the rational mind, the inhibition does not result in chaos, but in the apprehension of the Universe by means of a faculty to which the laws of the Reason do not apply; and when, returning to the normal state, we seek to analyse our experience, we find that the description abounds in rational absurdities.

On further consideration, however, it becomes gradually clear—gradually, because the habit of Trance must be firmly fixed before its fulminating impressions are truly intelligible—that there are not two kinds of Thought, or of Nature, but one only. The Law of the Mind is the sole substance of the Universe, as well as the sole means by which we apprehend it. There is thus no true antithesis between the conditions of Trance and those of ratiocination and perception; the fact that Trance is not amenable to the rules of argument is impertinent. We say that in Chess a Knight traverses the diagonal of a rectangle measuring three squares by two, neglecting its motion as a material object in space. We have described a definite limited relation in terms of a special sense which works by an arbitrary symbolism: when we analyse any example of our ordinary mental processes, we find the case entirely similar. For what we "see," "hear," *etc.*, depends upon our idiosyncrasies, for one thing, and upon conventional interpretation for another. Thus we agree to call grass green, and to avoid walking over the edge of precipices, without any attempt to make sure that any two minds have exactly identical conceptions of what these things may mean; and just so we agree upon the moves in Chess. By the rules of the game, then, we must think and act, or we risk every kind of error; but we may be perfectly well aware that the rules are arbitrary, and that it is after all only a game. The constant folly of the traditional mystic has been to be so proud of himself for discovering the great secret that the Universe is no more than a toy invented by himself for his amusement that he hastens to display his powers by deliberately misunderstanding and misusing the toy. He has not grasped the fact that just because it is no more than a projection of his own Point-of-View, it is integrally Himself that he offends!

Here lies the error of such Pantheism as that of Mansur el-Hallaj, whom Sir Richard Burton so delightfully twits (in the *Kasîdah*) with his impotence—

> Mansur was wise, but wiser they who
> smote him with the hurlèd stones;
> And though his blood a witness bore, no
> Wisdom-Might could mend his bones.

God was in the stones no less than within his tarband-wrapping; and when the twain crashed together, one point of perception of the fact was obscured—which was in no wise his design!

To us, however, this matter is not one for regret; it is (like every phenomenon) an Act of Love. And the very definition of such Act is the Passing Beyond of two Events into a Third, and their withdrawal into a Silence or Nothingness by simultaneous reaction. In this sense it may be said that the Universe is a constant issue into Trance; and in fact the proper understanding of any Event by means of the suitable Contemplation should produce the type of Trance appropriate to the complex Event-Individual in the case.

Now all Magick is useful to produce Trance; for (α) it trains the mind in the discipline necessary to Yoga; (β) it exalts the spirit to the impersonal and divine sublimity which is the first condition of success; (γ) it enlarges the scope of the mind, assuring it full mastery of every subtler plane of Nature, thus affording it adequate material for ecstatic consummation of the Eucharist of Existence.

The essence of the idea of Trance is indeed contained in that of Magick, which is preeminently the transcendental Science and Art. Its method is, in one chief sense, Love, the very key of Trance; and, in another, the passing beyond normal conditions. The verbs to transcend, to transmit, to transcribe, and their like, are all of cardinal virtue in Magick. Hence "Love is the law, love under will" is the supreme epitome of Magical doctrine, and its universal Formula. For need any man fear to state boldly that every Magical Operation soever is only complete when it is characterised (in one sense or another) by the occurrence of Trance. It was ill done to restrict the use of the word to the supersession of dualistic human consciousness by the impersonal and monistic state of Samadhi. Fast bubbles the fountain of Error from the morass of Ignorance when distinction is forcibly drawn "between any one thing and any other thing." Yea, verily, and Amen! it is the first necessity as it is the last attainment of Trance to abolish every form and every order of dividuality so fast as it presents itself. By this ray may ye read in the Book of your own Magical Record the authentic stigma of your own success.

Energy

ENERGY is the Sacramental Motive of Event: it is thus omnipresent, in manifestation by interruption and compensation and otherwise by the corresponding withdrawal. (In this connection let there be remembered the full formula of Tetragrammaton.)

There are, however, three main types of special experience which are noteworthy landmarks in the process of Initiation, and of urgent practical value to the Magician.

The symbol of the Sacrament being observed, they differ as do the three participants therein: the God, the Priest, and the Communicant.

In the highest, that is of Kether, the Energy radiates wholly from oneself: that is, one is entirely identified with Hadit.

In the middle, that of Chokmah, the Energy passes wholly through oneself: that is, one assumes the functions of Tahuti.

In the lowest, that is of Geburah, the Energy impinges wholly upon oneself: that is, one absorbs it as a man.

In all cases, the Energy of which it is here written is not particular or personified; it is Energy in itself, without quality.

The highest mode can only be fully apprehended by an Ipsissimus; it is the final attainment. It is the active counterpart of the higher form of the Beatific Vision.

The middle mode is proper to a Magus, or to one aspiring to his prophetic function. It is described, and the method of attaining it set forth, in the Book called *Opus Lutetianum*.

The lowest mode is the peculiar task of a Major Adept. It is best accomplished by means of the Secret of the Sanctuary of the Gnosis (IX° O.T.O.).

Of the highest mode it would be neither fit nor useful to treat more intimately: the middle mode concerns each Magician in his peculiar and private relations with the Infinite, and demands from each of its Adepts a special preoccupation: but of the lowest it is convenient to make further mention.

It is a strangely convincing proof of the true care of Nature for Her instruments, despite the superficial evidence to the contrary on which the doctrines of pessimism are based, that the most precious, the one ultimately essential Grace that can possibly be bestowed on mankind is, of all Magical benefit, that which may be attained with more ease and certainty than any other. For Energy is itself all that is: and we vary with the quantity and quality thereof, which we can call "ourselves."

The price which She demands is without doubt heavy enough for a certain class; but it is equally to be paid, in varying degree, for every type of Mystical and Magical Adventure.

This price is in essence the full Understanding of the Mind of Nature Herself, and complete sympathy with Her Way of Work. All the moral codes of mankind, for all their absurd diversities, have one common factor: they pretend to have found motives and methods which are superior to Hers.

That is, they presume a conception of the End which is beyond Her view: they assert the possession of an Intelligence loftier than that which has produced the Universe. Consider only that the highest manifestation possible to the rational mind is the discovery of the Laws which summarize Her manner of operation!

We may then say at once that all such pretentious arrogance is impudence and absurdity; and it must be surrendered, nay more, uprooted and calcined before any serious progress can be made in the Royal and Sacerdotal Art. Hence also any aspiration of a partial order, any which depends for its wisdom on the justice of our perceptions of our own needs, is almost certain to be tainted with the very poison of which Nature would purge us.

There is in fact only one Magical Operation of whose propriety we may always be sure; and that is the increase of our sum of Energy. It is even indiscreet to try to specify the kind of Energy required, and worse to consider any particular purpose.

Energy being increased, Nature will herself supply clarity: our Vision is obscure only because our Energy is deficient. For Energy is the Substance of the Universe. When it is adequate, we are in no doubt as to how to employ it; witness the evident case of the will of the Adolescent. It is also to be well noted that moral obstructions to the right use of this Energy cause at once the most hideous deformations of character, and determine the gravest lesions of the nervous system.

Let therefore the Magician divest himself of all preconceptions as to the nature of his True Will, but apply himself eagerly to increasing his Potential. In this discipline (morever) he is beginning to fit himself for that very abdication of *all that he has and all that he is* which is the essence of the Oath of the Abyss!

Thus then do we find one more of those paradoxes which are the images of the Truth of the Supernals: by destroying our own highest morality, and relying upon our natural instinct as the sole guide, we come unaware upon the most simple, and the most sublime, of all ethical and spiritual conceptions.

Knowledge

DAÄTH — Knowledge — is not a Sephira. It is not on the Tree of Life: that is, there is in reality no such thing.

Of this thesis there are many proofs. The simplest (if not the best) is perhaps as follows:

All knowledge may be expressed in the form S = P.

But if so, the idea P is really implicit in S; thus we have learnt nothing.

And, of course, if not so, the statement is simply false.

Now see how we come at once to paradox. For the thought "There is no such thing as knowledge," "Knowledge is a false idea," or however it may be phrased, can be expressed as S = P: it is itself a thing known.

In other words, the attempt to analyse the idea leads immediately to a muddle in the mind.

But this is of the essence of the Occult Wisdom concerning Daäth. For Daäth is the crown of the Ruach, the Intellect; and its place is in the Abyss. That is, it breaks into pieces immediately it is examined.

There is no coherence below the Abyss, or in it; to obtain this, which is one of the chief canons of Truth, we must reach Neschamah.

For this there is another explanation, quite apart from the purely logical trap. $S = P$ (unless identical, and therefore senseless) is an affirmation of duality; or, we may say, intellectual perception is a denial of Samadhic truth. It is therefore essentially false in the depths of its nature.

The simplest and most obvious statement will not bear analysis. "Vermilion is red" is undeniable, no doubt; but on inquiry it is found to be meaningless. For each term must be defined by means of at least two other terms, of which the same thing is true; so that the process of definition is always *"obscurum per obscurius."* For there are no truly simple terms. There is no real intellectual perception possible. What we suppose to be such is in fact a series of more or less plausible conventions based upon the apparent parallelism of experience. There is no final warrant that any two persons mean precisely the same thing by "sweet," or "high"; even such conceptions as those of number are perhaps only identical in relation to practical vulgar applications.

These and similar considerations lead to certain types of philosophical scepticism. Neschamic conceptions are nowise exempt from this criticism, for, even supposing them identical in any number of persons, their expression, being intellectual, will suffer the same stress as normal perceptions.

But none of this shakes, or even threatens, the Philosophy of Thelema. On the contrary, it may be called the Rock of its foundation. For the issue of all is evidently that all conceptions are necessarily unique because there can never be two identical points-of-view; and this corresponds with the facts; for there are points-of-view close kin, and thus there may be a superficial general agreement, as there is, which is found to be false on analysis, as has been shewn.

From the above it will be understood how it comes that there are no Trances of Knowledge; and this bids us enquire into the tradition of the Grimoires that all knowledge is miraculously attainable. The answer is that, while all Trances are Destroyers of Knowledge—since, for one thing, they all destroy the sense of Duality—they yet put into their Adept the means of knowledge. We may regard rational apprehension as a projection of Truth in dualistic form; so that he who possesses any given Truth has only to symbolise it in terms of the intellect to obtain its image in the form of Knowledge.

This conception is difficult; an illustration may clear its view. An architect can indicate the general characteristics of a building on paper by means of two drawings—a ground plan and an elevation. Neither but is false in nearly every respect; each is partial, each lacks depth, and so on. And yet, in combination, they do represent to the trained imagination what the building actually is; also, "illusions" as they are, no other illusions will serve the mind to discover the truth which they intend.

This is the reality hidden in all the illusions of the intellect; and this is the basis of the necessity for the Aspirant of having his knowledge accurate and adequate.

The common Mystic affects to despise Science as "illusion": this is the most fatal of all errors. For the instruments with which he works are all of this very order of "illusory things." We know that lenses distort images; but for all that, we can acquire information about distant objects which proves correct when the lens is constructed according to certain "illusory" principles and not by arbitrary caprice. The Mystic of this kind is generally recognized by men as a proud fool; he knows the fact, and is hardened in his presumption and arrogance. One finds him goaded by his subconscious shame to active attacks on Science; he gloats upon the apparent errors of calculation which constantly occur, not at all understanding the self-imposed limitations of validity of statement which are always implied; in short, he comes at last to abandon his own postulates, and takes refuge in the hermit-crab-carapace of the theologian.

But, on the other hand, to him who has firmly founded his rational thinking on sound principles, who has acquired deep comprehension of one fundamental science, and made proper paths between it and its germans which he understands only in general, who has, finally, secured the whole of this structure by penetrating through the appropriate Trances to the Neschamic Truths of which it is the rightly-ordered projection in the Ruach, to him the field of Knowledge, thus well-ploughed, well-sown, well-fertilized, well left to ripen; is ready for him to reap. The man who truly understands the underlying formulæ of one root-subject can easily extend his apprehension to the boughs, leaves, flowers, and fruit; and it is in this sense that the mediæval masters of Magick were justified in claiming that by the evocation of a given Daimon the worthy Octinomos might acquire the perfect knowledge of all sciences, speak with all tongues, command the love of all, or otherwise deal with all Nature as from the standpoint of its Maker. Crude are those credulous or critical who thought of the Evocation as the work of an hour or a week!

And the gain thereof to the Adept? Not the pure gold, *certes*, nor the Stone of the Philosophers! But yet a very virtuous weapon of much use on the Way; also, a mighty comfort to the human side of him; for the sweet fruit that hangs upon the Tree that makes men Gods is just this sun-ripe and soft-bloom-veiled globe of Knowledge.

Understanding

THE NATURE of Knowledge, the culmination and stasis of the Intellectual faculties, has been discussed in the previous essay. It implies a contradiction in terms. Understanding is the resolution of this antinomy. It is the chief quality of Neschamah, the Intelligence—an idea insusceptible of true definition because supra-rational, and only appreciable by direct experience. One can say, at most, that it is independent of any of the normal modes of motion of the mind.

(It is a significant illustration of the truth of this Qabalistic theory, that women often possess most excellent Intelligence, while totally incapable of the Knowledge and Reason on which, logically, it is founded.)

Samadhi, at first onset productive of bewildering Ecstasy, ultimates in this Understanding; one may say, therefore, that Understanding implies a certain Samadhic quality of apprehension. Duality is (perhaps) not absolutely abolished save in the superstructure of the state; but it assumes a form which it would be absurd to call dualistic.

(It will be noticed that violation of logic is essential to every true effort to convey the conception.)

This fact lies at the root of all Trinitarian symbolism; the scheme is geometrical in idea, and even arithmetical, as shewn by the attribution of Binah to the number 3. But the solution of every dyad in a Triune Triad is misleading, in so far as it purports to interpret the phenomenon in terms of intellect, and only useful as it may train the reasoning faculties to supersede themselves in a sublime suicide upon the Altar of the Mystic Intuition—though this, after all, is a mean imitation of the proper process. For it is, firstly, unscientific in method; and, secondly, illegitimate in its denial of its own validity.

The only correct and adequate mode of the Attainment of Understanding is to shut off and to inhibit the rational mind altogether, thus leaving a *Tabula rasa* upon which the entirely alien faculty—*de novo* and *sui generis*—can write its first word.

But then (it will surely be said) what is more unintelligent than this supposed Intelligence? Than this formless, even delirious Ecstasy which sweeps away all shapes of thought? No sane man would deny this premiss: but the explanation is that this Ecstasy is (so to say) the throe of Birth of the new faculty. It is surely natural for an observer to be startled, for the moment, by the discovery of a new Universe. Ananda must be mastered manfully, not indulged as a vice in the manner of the Mystic! Samadhi must be clarified by Sila, by the stern virtue of constraint: and then appears the paradox that the new Law of the Mind has "come not to destroy but to fulfil" the old. The Understanding takes full cognizance of all that vast material which the Reason was unable to build into any coherent structure. The contradictions have disappeared by absorption; they have been accepted as essential factors in the nature of Truth, which without them were a mere congeries of Facts.

It will be clear from all these considerations that there need be no surprise at this primordial paradox: that Scepticism, absolute in every dimension, is the sole possible basis of true Attainment. All attempts to shirk the issue by appeals to "faith," by mystic transcendental sophistries, or any other spiritual varieties of the Three-Card-Trick, are devoted to the most abject destruction.

One cannot "find the Lady" by any other way than that of the Knight-Errant, of the Great Fool—the Way of the Eagle in the Air—whose Sacred Number is the Sacred Zero. Yea also, Naught being All, and All being Pan, the only due address to Godhead is in the dual form παμφαγε πανγενετωρ.*

For all must be destroyed that All may be begotten.

---

* ["all-devourer, all-begetter"]

Chastity

THOSE WORKS of Ancient and Mediæval Literature which more particularly concern the Seeker after Truth, concur on one point. The most worthless Grimoires of Black Magic, no less than the highest philosophical flights of the Brotherhood which we name not, insist upon the virtue of Chastity as cardinal to the Gate of Wisdom.

Let first be noted this word Virtue, the quality of Manhood, integral with Virility. The Chastity of the Adept of the Rose and Cross, or of the Graal-Knights of Monsalvat, is not other than very opposite to that of which the poet can write:

> ... Chastity that slavering sates
> His lust without the walls, mews, and is gone,
> Preening himself that his lewd lips relent.

Or to that emasculate frigor of Alfred Tennyson and the Academic Schools.

The Chastity whose Magical Energy both protects and urges the aspirant to the Sacred Mysteries is quite contrary in its deepest nature to all vulgar ideas of it; for it is, in the first place, a positive passion; in the second, connected only by obscure magical links with the sexual function; and, in the third, the deadliest enemy of every form of bourgeois morality and sentiment.

It may assist us to create in our minds a clear concept of this noblest and rarest— yet most necessary—of the Virtues, if we draw the distinction between it and one of its ingredients, Purity.

Purity is a passive or at least static quality; it connotes the absence of all alien admixture from any given idea; as, pure gallium, pure mathematics, pure race. It is a secondary and derived use of the word which we find in such expressions as "pure milk," which imply freedom from contamination.

Chastity, *per contra*, as the etymology (*castus,* possibly connected with *castrum*, a fortified camp[*]) suggests, may be supposed to assert the moral attitude of readiness to resist any assault upon an existing state of Purity.

> So dear to heaven is saintly chastity
> That when a soul is found sincerely so
> A thousand liveried angels lackey it,

sang Milton, with the true poet's veil-piercing sword-vision; for service is but waste unless action demands it.

---

[*] The root *cas* means house; and an house is *Beth*, the letter of Mercury, the Magus of the Tarot. He is not still, in a place of repose, but the quintessence of all Motion. He is the Logos; and He is phallic. This doctrine is of the utmost Qabalistic importance.

The Sphinx is not to be mastered by holding aloof; and the brutish innocence of Paradise is always at the mercy of the Serpent. It is his Wisdom that should guard our Ways; we need his swiftness, subtlety, and his royal prerogative of dealing death.

The Innocence of the Adept? We are at once reminded of the strong Innocence of Harpocrates, and of His Energy of Silence. A chaste man is thus not merely one who avoids the contagion of impure thoughts and their results, but whose virility is competent to restore Perfection to the world about him. Thus the Parsifal who flees from Kundry and her attendant flower-witches loses his way and must wander long years in the Desert; he is not truly chaste until he is able to redeem her, an act which he performs by the reunion of the Lance and the Sangraal.

Chastity may thus be defined as the strict observance of the Magical Oath; that is, in the Light of the Law of Thelema, absolute and perfected devotion to the Holy Guardian Angel and exclusive pursuit of the Way of the True Will.

It is entirely incompatible with the cowardice of moral attitude, the emasculation of soul and stagnation of action, which commonly denote the man called chaste by the vulgar.

"Beware of abstinence from action!" is it not written in Our lection? For the nature of the Universe being Creative Energy, aught else blasphemes the Goddess, and seeks to introduce the elements of a real death within the pulses of Life.

The chaste man, the true Knight-Errant of the Stars, imposes continually his essential virility upon the throbbing Womb of the King's Daughter; with every stroke of his Spear he penetrates the heart of Holiness, and bids spring forth the Fountain of the Sacred Blood, splashing its scarlet dew throughout Space and Time. His Innocence melts with its white-hot Energy the felon fetters of that Restriction which is Sin, and his Integrity with its fury of Righteousness establishes that Justice which alone can satisfy the yearning lust of the Womanhood whose name is Opportunity. As the function of the *castrum* or *castellum* is not merely to resist a siege, but to compel to Obedience of Law and Order every pagan within range of its riders, so also it is the Way of Chastity to do more than defend its purity against assault. For he is not wholly pure who is imperfect; and perfect is no man in himself without his fulfillment in all possibility. Thus then must he be instant to seek all proper adventure and achieve it, seeing well to it that by no means should such distract him or divert his purpose, polluting his true Nature and hamstringing his true Will.

Woe, woe therefore to him the unchaste who shirks scornful the seeming-trivial, or flees fearful the desperate, adventure. And woe, thrice woe, and four times woe be to him who is allured by the adventure, slacking his Will and demitted from his Way: for as the laggard and the dastard are lost, so is the toy of circumstance dragged down to nethermost Hell.

Sir Knight, be vigilant: watch by your arms and renew your Oath; for that day is of sinister augury and deadly charged with danger which ye fill not to overflowing with gay deeds and bold of masterful, of manful Chastity!

Silence

O F ALL the Magical and Mystical Virtues, of all the Graces of the Soul, of all the Attainments of the Spirit, none has been so misunderstood, even when at all apprehended, as Silence.

It would not be possible to enumerate the common errors: nay, it may be said that to think of it at all is in itself an error; for its nature is Pure Being, that is to say, Nothing, so that it is beyond all intellection or intuition. Thus then the utmost of our Essay can be only a certain Wardenship, as it were a Tyling of the Lodge wherein the Mystery of Silence may be consummated.

For this attitude there is sound traditional authority; for Harpocrates, God of Silence, is called "The Lord of Defence and Protection."

But His nature is by no means that negative and passive silence which the word commonly connotes; for He is the All-Wandering Spirit; the Pure and Perfect Knight-Errant, who answers all Enigmas, and opens the Closed Portal of the King's Daughter. But Silence in the vulgar sense is not the answer to the Riddle of the Sphinx; it is that which is created by that answer. For Silence is the Equilibrium of Perfection; so that Harpocrates is the omniform, the universal Key to every Mystery soever. The Sphinx is the "Puzzel or Pucelle," the Feminine Idea to which there is only one complement, always different in form, and always identical in essence. This is the signification of the Gesture of the God; it is shewn more clearly in His adult form as the Fool of the Tarot and as Bacchus Diphues, and without equivocation when He appears as Baphomet.

When we inquire more closely into His symbolism, the first quality which engages our attention is doubtless His innocence. Not without deep wisdom is He called twin of Horus; and this is the Æon of Horus: it is He who sent forth Aiwass His minister to proclaim its advent. The Fourth Power of the Sphinx is Silence; to us then who aspire to this power as the crown of our Work, it will be of utmost value to attain His innocence in all its fullness. We must understand first of all that the root of Moral Responsibility, on which Man stupidly prides himself as distinguishing him from the other animals, is Restriction, which is the Word of Sin. Indeed, there is truth in the Hebrew fable, that the knowledge of Good and Evil brings forth Death. To regain Innocence is to regain Eden. We must learn to live without the murderous consciousness that every breath we draw swells the sails which bear our frail vessels to the Port of the Grave. We must cast out Fear by Love; seeing that Every Act is an Orgasm, their total issue cannot be but Birth. Also, Love is the law: thus every act must be Righteousness and Truth. By certain Meditations this may be understood and established; and this ought to be done so thoroughly that we become unconscious of our Sanctification, for only then is Innocence made perfect. This state is, in fact, a necessary condition of any proper contemplation of what we are accustomed to consider the first task of the Aspirant, the solution of the question, "What is my True Will?" For until we become innocent, we are certain to try to judge our Will by some Canon of what seems "right" or "wrong"; in other words, we are apt to criticise our Will from the outside, whereas True Will should spring, a fountain of Light, from within, and flow unchecked, seething with Love, into the Ocean of Life.

This is the true idea of Silence; it is our Will which issues, perfectly elastic, sublimely Protean, to fill every interstice of the Universe of Manifestation which it meets in its course. There is no gulf too great for its immeasurable strength, no strait too arduous for its imperturbable subtlety. It fits itself with perfect precision to every need; its fluidity is the warrant of its fidelity. Its form is always varied by that of the particular imperfection which it encounters: its essence is identical in every event. And always the effect of its action is Perfection, that is, Silence; and this Perfection is ever the same, being perfect, yet ever different, because each case presents its own peculiar quantity and quality.

It is impossible for inspiration itself to sound a dithyramb of Silence; for each new aspect of Harpocrates is worthy of the music of the Universe throughout Eternity. I have simply been led by my loyal Love of that strange Race among whom I find myself incarnate to indite this poor stanza of the infinite Epic of Harpocrates as being the facet of His fecund Brilliance which has refracted the most needful light upon mine own darkling Entrance to His shrine of fulminating, of ineffable Godhead.

I praise the luxuriant Rapture of Innocence, the virile and pantomorphous Ecstasy of all-Fulfilment; I praise the Crowned and Conquering Child whose name is Force and Fire, whose subtlety and strength make sure serenity, whose Energy and Endurance accomplish the Attainment of the Virgin of the Absolute; who, being manifested, is the Player upon the sevenfold pipe, the Great God Pan, and, being withdrawn into the Perfection that he willed, is Silence.

Love

*And the Magus is Love, and bindeth together
That and This in His Conjuration.*

THE FORMULA of Tetragrammaton is the complete mathematical expression of Love. Its essence is this: any two things unite, with a double effect; firstly, the destruction of both, accompanied by the ecstasy due to the relief of the strain of separateness; secondly, the creation of a third thing, accompanied by the ecstasy of the realisation of existence, which is Joy until with development it becomes aware of its imperfection, and loves.

This formula of Love is universal; all the laws of Nature are its servitors. Thus, gravitation, chemical affinity, electrical potential, and the rest—and these are alike mere aspects of the general law—are so many differently-observed statements of the unique tendency.

The Universe is conserved by the duplex action involved in the formula. The disappearance of Father and Mother is precisely compensated by the emergence of Son and Daughter. It may therefore be considered as a perpetual-motion-engine which continually develops rapture in each of its phases.

The sacrifice of Iphigenia at Aulis may be taken as typical of the formula: the mystical effect is the assumption of the maid to the bosom of the goddess; while, for the magical, the destruction of her earthly part, the fawn, composes the rage of Æolus, and bids the Danaids set sail.

Now it cannot be too clearly understood, or too acutely realised by means of action, that the intensity of the Joy liberated varies with the original degree of opposition between the two elements of the union. Heat, light, electricity are phenomena expressive of the fullness of passion, and their value is greatest when the diversity of the Energies composing the marriage is most strenuous. One obtains more from the explosion of Hydrogen and Oxygen than from the dull combination of substances indifferent to each other. Thus, the union of Nitrogen and Chlorine is so little satisfying to either molecule, that the resulting compound disintegrates with explosive violence at the slightest shock. We might say, then, in the language of Thelema, that such an act of love is not "love under will." It is, so to speak, a black magical operation.

Let us consider, in a figure, the "feelings" of a molecule of Hydrogen in the presence of one of Oxygen or of Chlorine. It is made to suffer intensely by the realisation of the extremity of its deviation from the perfect type of monad by the contemplation of an element so supremely opposed to its own nature at every point. So far as it is egoist, its reaction must be scorn and hatred; but as it understands the true shame that is put upon its separateness by the presence of its opposite, these feelings turn to anguished yearning. It begins to crave the electric spark which will enable it to assuage its pangs by the annihilation of all those properties which constitute its separate existence, in the rapture of union, and at the same time to fulfil its passion to create a perfect type of Peace.

We see the same psychology everywhere in the physical world. A stronger and more elaborate illustration might well have been drawn, were the purpose of this essay less catholic, from the structure of the atoms themselves, and their effort to resolve the agony of their agitation in the beatific Nirvana of the "noble" gases.

The process of Love under Will is evidently progressive. The Father who has slain himself in the womb of the Mother finds himself again, with her, and transfigured, in the Son. This Son acts as a new Father; and it is thus that the Self is constantly aggrandized, and able to counterpoise an ever greater Not-Self, until the final act of Love under Will which comprehends the Universe in Sammasamadhi.

The passion of Hatred is thus really directed against oneself; it is the expression of the pain and shame of separateness; and it only appears to be directed against the opposite by psychological transference. This thesis the School of Freud has made sufficiently clear.

There is then little indeed in common between Love and such tepid passions as regard,
affection, or kindliness; it is the uninitiate, who,
to his damnation in a hell of cabbage soup and
soap-suds, confuses them.

Love may best be defined as the passion of
Hatred inflamed to the point of madness, when
it takes refuge in Self-destruction.

Love is clear-sighted with the lust of deadly
rage, anatomizing its victim with keen energy,
seeking where best to strike home mortally to
the heart; it becomes blind only when its fury
has completely overpowered it, and thrust it into
the red maw of the furnace of self-immolation.

We must further distinguish Love in this
magical sense from the sexual formula, symbol
and type though that be thereof. For the pure
essence of Magick is a function of ultimate
atomic consciousness, and its operations must
be refined from all confusion and contamination. The truly magical operations of Love are
therefore the Trances, more especially those
of Understanding; as will readily have been
appreciated by those who have made a careful
Qabalistic study of the nature of Binah. For She
is omniform as Love and as Death, the Great
Sea whence all Life springs, and whose black
womb re-absorbs all. She thus resumes in herself the duplex process of the Formula of Love
under Will; for is not Pan the All-Begetter in the
heart of the Groves at high noon, and is not Her

"hair the trees of Eternity" the filaments of All-Devouring Godhead "under the Night of Pan"?

Yet let it not be forgotten that though She be love, her function is but passive; she is the vehicle of the Word, of Chokmah, Wisdom, the All-Father, who is the Will of the All-One. And thus they err with grievous error and dire who prate of Love as the Formula of Magick; Love is unbalanced, void, vague, undirected, sterile, nay, more, a very Shell, the prey of abject orts demonic: Love must be *under will.*

Truth

W HAT is Truth? It is absurd to attempt to define it, for when we say that S is P, rather than S is Q, or S is R, we assume that we already know the meaning of Truth. This is really why all the discussions as to whether Truth depends on external correspondence, internal coherence, or what not, neither produce conviction, nor withstand analysis. Briefly, Truth is an idea of a supra-rational order, pertaining to Neschamah, not to Ruach. That all rational conceptions imply that we know Truth, and that Truth is in their propositions, only shows that these so-called rational ideas are not really rational at all. Truth is by no means the only idea that resists rational analysis. There are very many ideas that remain indefinable: all simple ideas do so. At the back of all our efforts is the dead wall that we must already know what we are pretending to find out.

Consider the statement of the Angel in the 5th Æthyr in *The Vision and the Voice*:

> . . . all the symbols are interchangeable, for each one containeth in itself its own opposite. And this is the great Mystery of the Supernals that are beyond the Abyss. For below the Abyss, contradiction is division; but above the

> Abyss, contradiction is Unity. And there could
> be nothing true except by virtue of the contra-
> diction that is contained in itself.

When that was given to the Master Therion,
how obscure a saying and hard that seemed to
him! Yet in the light of the above paragraphs,
how simply obvious the proposition has become, and how far short of—Truth!

What then can be meant by the title of this
compilation: "Little Essays toward Truth"?
Do we not all assume a perfectly illogical
conception of Truth as an entity of "the supra-
mundane order, whence a whirling flame and
flying Light subsist"? Do we not instinctively
assimilate these ideas of Truth and Light,
though there is no rational nexus? Is it not clear,
then, that we do understand each other perfectly, so far as we can understand each other
at all, in a sphere such as Zoroaster calls "Intelligible," which "subsisteth beyond Mind" but
which we should "seek to grasp with the Flower
of Mind"? Must we not then assent to that other
Oracle, in which that Magus most sublime
asserts:

> For the King of all previously placed before the
> polymorphous World a Type, intellectual,
> incorruptible, the imprint of whose form is
> sent forth through the World, by which the
> Universe shone forth decked with Ideas all-
> various, of which the foundation is One, One
> and alone. From this the others rush forth,

distributed and separated through the various bodies of the Universe, and are borne in swarms through its vast abysses, ever whirling forth in illimitable radiation.

They are intellectual conceptions from the Paternal Fountain partaking abundantly of the brilliance of Fire in the culmination of unresting Time.

But the primary self-perfect Fountain of the Father poured forth these primogenial Ideas.

(It is to be remembered that the *Oracles of Zoroaster* continually proclaim in words of boundless brilliancy the doctrine here set forth: these Essays are indeed a species of Commentary thereupon, and I may say that I only came to understand them as perfectly as I now do in the course of this writing.)

Now this same Truth, which is Light, which is implicit in each spark of the Intelligible; what is it but the Self of Everyman? It is this that informs his every motion, this that lies closest to his heart and soul, being indeed their mainspring and their dial, the principle of section and of measure.

Now Initiation is, by etymology, the *journeying inwards;* it is the Voyage of Discovery (oh Wonder-World!) of one's own Soul. And this is Truth that stands upon the prow, eternally alert; this is Truth that sits with one strong hand gripping the helm!

Truth is our Path, and Truth is our Goal; ay! there shall came to all a moment of great Light when the Path is seen to be itself the Goal; and in that hour every one of us shall exclaim:

"I AM THE WAY, THE TRUTH, AND THE LIFE!"

Yea, the Life also, Life eternal in Time and boundless in Space; for what is Life but the continual resolution of the antimony of the diverse by the spasm of Love under Will, that is, by the constantly explosive, the orgiastic, perception of Truth, the dissolution of dividuality in one radiant star of Truth that ever revolveth, and goeth, and filleth the Heavens with Light?

I beseech you earnestly, dear Brethren, to grapple manfully as mighty wrestlers with the ideas in these Little Essays: to understand them—

> ... with the extended flame of far-reaching Mind, measuring all things except that Intelligible. But it is requisite to understand this; for if thou inclinest thy Mind thou wilt understand it, not earnestly; but it is becoming to bring with thee a pure and inquiring sense, to extend the void mind of thy soul to that Intelligible, that thou mayst learn the Intelligible, because it subsisteth beyond Mind.

For thus not only will you develop the spiritual intuition, the very Neschamah of your divine Being, but (in the degree of your Concentration, of your power to slow down and finally to stop the irritable movements of your ratiocinative machinery) to transmute these Essays—the *Prima Materia* of your Great Work; passing them through the stage of the Black Dragon, in which your rational ideas are wholly destroyed and putrefied, you will succeed in enflaming them in the fierce Furnace of your Creative Wills, until all things burn up together into one blazing mass of living, of relentless Light.

And thus come ye to Sammasamadhi — thus are ye free for ever of all the bonds that bound your Godhead!

> A similar Fire flashingly extending through the rushings of Air, or a Fire formless whence cometh the Image of a Voice, or even a flashing Light abounding, revolving, whirling forth, crying aloud. Also there is the Vision of the fire-flashing Courser of Light, or else a Child, borne aloft on the shoulders of the Celestial Steed, fiery, or clothed with gold, or naked, or shooting with the bow shafts of Light, and standing on the shoulders of the horse; then if thy meditation prolongeth itself, thou shalt unite all these Symbols into the Form of a Lion.

Then shall ye understand what is Truth, for ye shall understand your Selves, and YE ARE TRUTH!

Glossary

A

ABHIDHAMMA. The collection of treatises which embody the metaphysics of the Buddhist philosophy.

AHAMKARA. The Ego-making faculty.

ANANDA. Bliss.

ASANA. Posture. Any correct position of holding the body.

ATZILUTHIC WORLD. The Archetypal World that gave birth to three other worlds, each containing a repetition of the Sephiroth, but in a descending scale of brightness. See Diagram.

B

BABALON. Our Lady, See *Equinox* I(5), *The Vision and the Voice*.

BETH. Second letter of the Hebrew Alphabet. It is the letter of Wisdom, Magick, Mercury.

BHAGAVADGITA. Sacred hymn of the Vedanta Philosophy, translated by Sir Edwin Arnold in *The Song Celestial*.

BINAH. Understanding. The Third "Emanation" of the Absolute. The first "He" of the Tetragrammaton, the "Mother" in the Trinity. See Diagram.

C

CHIAH. The Creative impulse or Will. The second principle of the Fivefold constitution of man. See Diagram.

CHOKMAH. Wisdom. The Second "Emanation" of the Absolute, the "Yod" of Tetragrammaton, the "Father" in the Trinity. See Diagram.

CHORONZON. See *Equinox* I(5), *The Vision and the Voice*, 10th Æthyr.

CITY OF THE PYRAMIDS. Binah, the third Sephira, referred to Saturn. The final destruction of the knowledge of Daäth opens the gate of the City of the Pyramids. See *The Vision and the Voice*.

D
DAÄTH. Knowledge, child of Chokmah and Binah in one sense, in the other the empty and structureless condition of Choronzon.

E
EXEMPT ADEPT. Grade 7°=4°. which refers to Chesed, a correspondence of Jupiter. See Diagram.

G
GEBURAH. Strength; the Fifth "Emanation" of the Absolute. The Sephira of Mars. See Diagram.

H
HADIT. The infinitely small and atomic yet omnipresent point. See *Liber Legis, Equinox* I(7), also *Liber 555*.

HARPOCRATES. The Egyptian God of Silence, the babe in the egg. (The image of the concealed Father.) The Lord of Defence and Protection. See 777.

HORUS. In Egyptian cosmogony, the child of Isis and Osiris. The true Magick of Horus requires the passionate Union of opposites. The new Æon of

Horus. The Crowned and Conquering Child. See *Magick*.

I

IPSISSIMUS. Grade $10° = 1^\square$. Is beyond all comprehension of those of lower degrees.

J

JECHIDAH. The quintessential principle of the soul. One principle of the fivefold constitution of man. See Diagram.

K

KARMA. That which is made. The law of cause and effect, see "Science and Buddhism," Crowley's *Collected Works,* Vol. 2.

KETHER. The Crown. The First "Emanation" of the Absolute. Kether is in Malkuth and Malkuth is in Kether, but after another manner, Malkuth reflects Kether, for that which is above is like that which is below, and that which is below is like that which is above. See Diagram.

M

MAGICK. The science and art of causing change to occur in conformity with the Will. See *Magick in Theory and Practice,* by the Master Therion.

MAGUS. A Magician; also, technically, a Master of the Grade $9° = 2^\square$. The highest grade which it is ever possible to manifest in any way whatever upon this plane. Attains to Wisdom, declares his law, and is the Master of all Magick in its greatest and highest sense. See *Equinox* I(7), *Liber I,* and elsewhere.

MAJOR ADEPT. A grade of Adeptship. $6° = 5°$. Obtains a general mastery of all practical Magick, though without full comprehension. See *Equinox* I(1,3).

N

NESCHAMAH. Intuition. Aspiration. Intelligence. The Third principle of the fivefold constitution of man. See Diagram.

NEPHESCH. The "Animal Soul" of man, senses, emotion. The Fifth principle of the fivefold constitution of man. See Diagram.

NUIT. Infinite Space. See *Liber Legis* and *Equinox* I(7), p. 11.

O

OSIRIS. The Ancient Egyptian Redeemer, father of Horus.

OCTINOMOS. Master Magician.

P

PYRAMIDS, THE CITY OF THE. Binah, the Third Sephira, referred to Saturn. The final destruction of the knowledge of Daäth opens the gate of the City of Pyramids. See *The Vision and the Voice*.

Q

QABALAH. "The Tradition of the Secret Wisdom of the Hebrews." See *Equinox* I(5).

R

RUACH. The Intellect and other mental qualities. Reason. The Fourth principle of the fivefold constitution of man. See *777*, and Diagram.

S

SABBÈ PI DUKKHAM. "Everything is sorrow."

SAMADHI. Ecstasy or Super-consciousness. Etymologically: "Together with the Lord."

SAMMASAMADHI. Right Samadhi.

SEPHIROTH. The Tree of Life. See "Temple of Solomon," *Equinox* I(5). The *Sepher Sephiroth*, the Book of Emanations, describes the gradual evolution of the Deity from negative into positive existence. See *Equinox* I(8) (Supplement), and Diagram.

SILA. Virtue.

T

TAROT. The Book of Thoth, a pictorial epitome of the Ancient Initiated Wisdom. A method of Divination based on the Qabalistic Tree of Life.

TETRAGRAMMATON. Yod, He, Vau, Hé; The Ineffable Name (Jehovah) of the Hebrews. See Diagram.

THELEMA. Will. The word of the Law.

TIPHARETH. Beauty or Harmony, the Sixth "Emanation" of the Absolute. The Sephira harmonising and mediating between Kether and Malkuth. See Diagram.

Y

YOGA. Union. Between the subject and object, in consciousness; the soul and god, *etc.*, according to context.

Bibliography

Abhidhamma-pitika (London: Pali Text Society, 1900–69).

Bhagavadgita, ed. Daniel H. H. Ingalls, Harvard Oriental Series (Cambridge: Harvard U.P., 1953).

BURTON, SIR FRANCIS RICHARD. *The Kasidah of Haji Abdu el-Yezdi [pseud.] :* (London: B. Quaritch, 1880).

CROWLEY, ALEISTER AND DESTI, MARY. *Book 4.* 2 vols., Part I: Meditation; Part II: Magick (Theory) (London: Wieland, 1911-12). Reprinted in one volume as *Book Four* (York Beach: Weiser, 1980); see also *Magick,* ed. J. Symonds and K. Grant (Weiser, 1974).

CROWLEY, ALEISTER. *The Collected Works of Aleister Crowley,* 3 vols., ed. I. Back (Foyers: S.P.R.T., 1905-7). Reprinted (Homewood, IL: n.d., Yogi Publication Society).

_____. *The Equinox* I(1-10) (London: v.p., 1909-1913, reprinted New York: Weiser, 1972); selections in *Gems from the Equinox* (q.v.).

_____. *The Equinox* III(1) (Detroit: Universal, 1919, reprinted New York: Weiser, 1972); selections in *Gems from the Equinox* (q.v.)

_____. *[Equinox* III(3).] *The Equinox of the Gods* (London: O.T.O., 1936).

_____. *[Equinox* III(4).] *Eight Lectures on Yoga* (London: O.T.O., 1939, reprinted Falcon, 1985).

_____. *[Equinox* III(5).] *The Book of Thoth* (London: O.T.O., 1944, reprinted Weiser, 1989).

_____. *[Equinox* III(9).] *The Holy Books of Thelema* (York Beach: Weiser, 1983, reprinted 1989).

_____. *The Equinox* III(10) (New York: Thelema, 1986, reprinted York Beach: Weiser, 1990).

_____. *Gems from the Equinox,* ed. I. Regardie (St. Paul: Llewellyn, 1974, reprinted Las Vegas: Falcon, 1989).

_____. *Konx Om Pax: Essays in Light* (London: S.P.R.T. and New York: Walter Scott, 1907); facsimile edition by Teitan Press (Chicago, 1990).

_____. *[Liber I.] Liber B vel Magi sub figura I.* In *The Equinox* I(7) (q.v.) and *Magick in Theory and Practice* (q.v.); also in *Gems from the Equinox* (q.v.), *Equinox* III(9) and III(10) (q.v.).

_____. *[Liber LXV.] Liber Cordis Cincte Serpente sub figura LXV.* In Θελημα (q.v.); *The Equinox* III(1) and III(9) (q.v.).

_____. *[Liber 418, The Vision and the Voice.] Liber XXX Ærum Vel Sæculi Sub figura CDXVIII.* First published in *The Equinox* I(5), suppl. (q.v.); with commentary, ed. K. J. Germer (Barstow: Thelema Publishing Co., 1952); with abridged commentary, ed. I. Regardie (Dallas: Sangreal, 1972); in *Gems from the Equinox* (q.v.).

_____. *[Liber 555.] Liber Had sub figura DLV.* In *The Equinox* I(7) (q.v.); also in *Gems from the Equinox* (q.v.).

_____. *[Liber 777.] 777* (London: privately printed, 1909); with additions as *777 Revised* (London: Neptune, 1955); see also *777 and Other Qabalistic Writings* (York Beach: Weiser, 1985).

_____. *Magick in Theory and Practice* (Paris: Lecram, 1929, reprinted New York: Dover, 1976); see also *Magick*, ed. J. Symonds and K. Grant (Weiser, 1974).

_____. *[Opus Lutetianum.] Liber CDXIV, The Book of the High Magick Art [The Paris Working].* In *Sex and Religion*, ed. M. Motta (Nashville: Thelema Publishing Co., 1981).

_____. Θελημα (London: privately printed, 1909).

JULIANUS. *The Chaldean Oracles*, ed. & trans. Ruth Majercik (Leiden & New York: E.J. Brill, 1989).

_____. *The Chaldæan Oracles as set down by Julianus*, trans. F. Patrizzi & T. Stanley (Gillette, NJ: Heptangle Books, 1989).

JUVENAL. *Saturæ*, ed. W. V. Clausen (Oxford: Clarendon Press, 1959).

Liber AL vel Legis sub figura CCXX. [The Book of the Law.] First published in Θελημα (q.v.); also in *The Equinox* I(7) (q.v.); in *Equinox* III(3) (q.v.); as *The Book of the Law* (London & Pasadena: O.T.O., 1938); see also *The Book of the Law* (Kings Beach: Thelema Publications, 1981) and (York Beach: Weiser, 1987); also in *The Equinox* III(9) and III(10) (q.v.). Numerous other editions.

ZOROASTER. *Oracula Magica Zorastris cum Platonis et Pselli nunc.* Primum editi. E Bibliotheca regia. Studio Johannis Opsopoei. Parisiis, 1607.

_____. *The Chaldæan Oracles of Zoroaster*, ed. W. Westcott (London: Theosophical Pub. Soc., 1895) (Collecteana Hermetica, Vol. 6).

Index